Brian Wildsmith's WILD ANIMALS

A herd of reindeer

For Simon

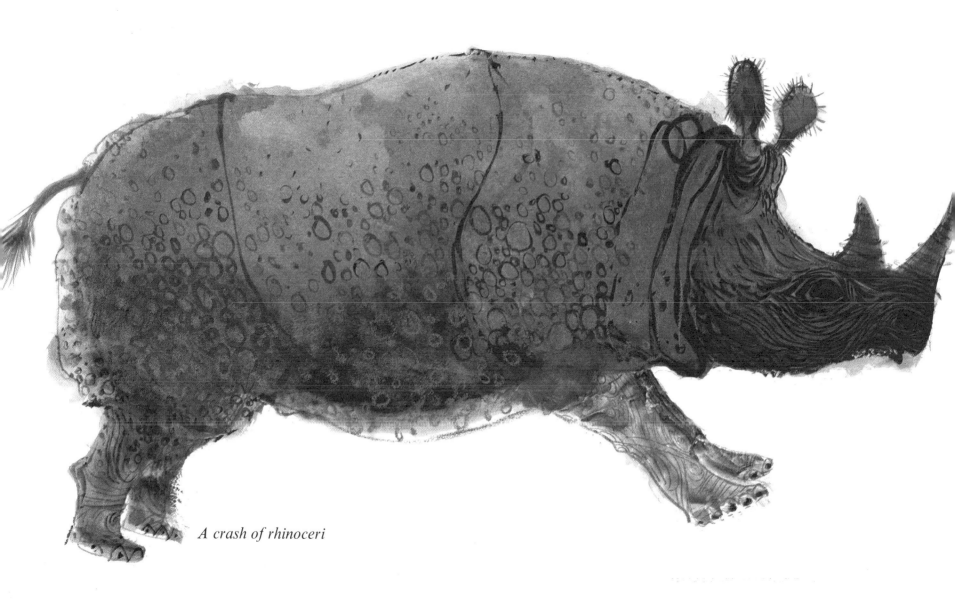

A crash of rhinoceri

Beasts, more than one in number

If a solitary elephant stirs wonder in the beholder, two seem twice as wonderful. A pair. A team? That depends on what they are doing. If it is work, then beyond doubt they form a team. But if, as in Kipling's story, the elephants are watching their child, they are a couple. How about more than two—a whole batch, a group, a crowd? To the zoo keeper, the circus master, and the man whose teak they lift into piles, all those elephants moving in concert are a *herd*.

For most of us, even if we entertain no hope of owning an elephant, the names and labels for groups of animals have appeal. Part of the fun lies in noting which beasts carry the same names for their gatherings or companies. Besides elephants and camels, whom man trains to his service, the wild deer and the almost vanished North American buffalo travel as herds. So do such farm animals as sheep, goats, pigs, horses, cows, and cattle generally. Certain sea creatures do, too; whales, for instance, belong to herds, as do porpoises and sharks, though each of these species has still another name for its group, its band, its gang. J. Donald Adams, literary editor emeritus of the *New York Times*, comments in an essay called ''A Shrewdness of Apes'' (we have a picture of *a shrewdness of apes* in this book) that it would be incongruous to use the term *herd* for animals no larger than a dog; if we spoke of ''a herd of mice'', everyone would laugh, he implies. Yet, in a phrase hard to forget, Shakespeare raised these little quarry to herd size for a minute when he called them ''mice and rats and *such small deer*.''

Usually the word *flock* serves for domestic beasts that move in a herd—the flock of sheep, goats, hogs, and swine of whatever sort; but it has too peaceable a sound for the wild ones, the boars, the fierce Arkansas razorbacks, the javelinas who go in *drifts* and *droves*.

Flock labels most assemblies of feathered creatures: geese, pigeons, hens, turkeys, and other kinds of birds. In water, however, geese assume their own special name; they become *a gaggle of geese*. Turkeys a-roosting make a *rafter* of turkeys. Song and game birds call up a more poetic image than turkeys; they may be winging with the early sun as *an exaltation* or *an ascension* of larks, unless they happen to be a *murmuration* of starlings, a *fall* of wood-cock, or possibly a *covey* of partridge.

But of tigers, expect no flocks or herds or droves. Tigers are "loners;" not for them the chumminess of numbers. An *ambush* of tigers better suits their nature. As for lions, even though explorers like the Carl Akeleys have seen them napping in the African tall grass—a whole *clowder* lying on their backs with four feet up in the air—lions are never just a flock. In unison, gloriously, they form a *pride* of lions. As for *clowder*, the term refers to house-cats.

Scattered through dictionaries, the elusive words that mean "creatures assembled" may be tracked down. Old books on game hunting and fishing yield odd group names, some of them proof of the ingenuity or wit of a Nimrod long gone. It is not hard to understand why the furtive foxes, stealing to a local hennery were called a *skulk* of foxes; nor why when certain great armored monsters threshed through the bush, a listening hunter reckoned their unseen number simply as a *crash* of rhinoceri. Less obvious in origin, but equally fascinating are a *route* of wolves, a *lepe* of leopards, a *sloth* of bears (slowly rousing from a winter's sleep?), and a cete of badgers. A *cete*, exotic though it looks, is only a country-man's way of writing a *set*, back in a time when everyone spelled as he pleased. And a set of badgers has the same attractiveness as a *family* of otters or a *nursery* of raccoons—the beauty of young and old living together contentedly.

Brian Wildsmith's WILD ANIMALS

FRANKLIN WATTS, INC.
575 LEXINGTON AVENUE, NEW YORK, N.Y. 10022

watts
international

A sloth of bears

A nursery of racoons

An ambush
of tigers

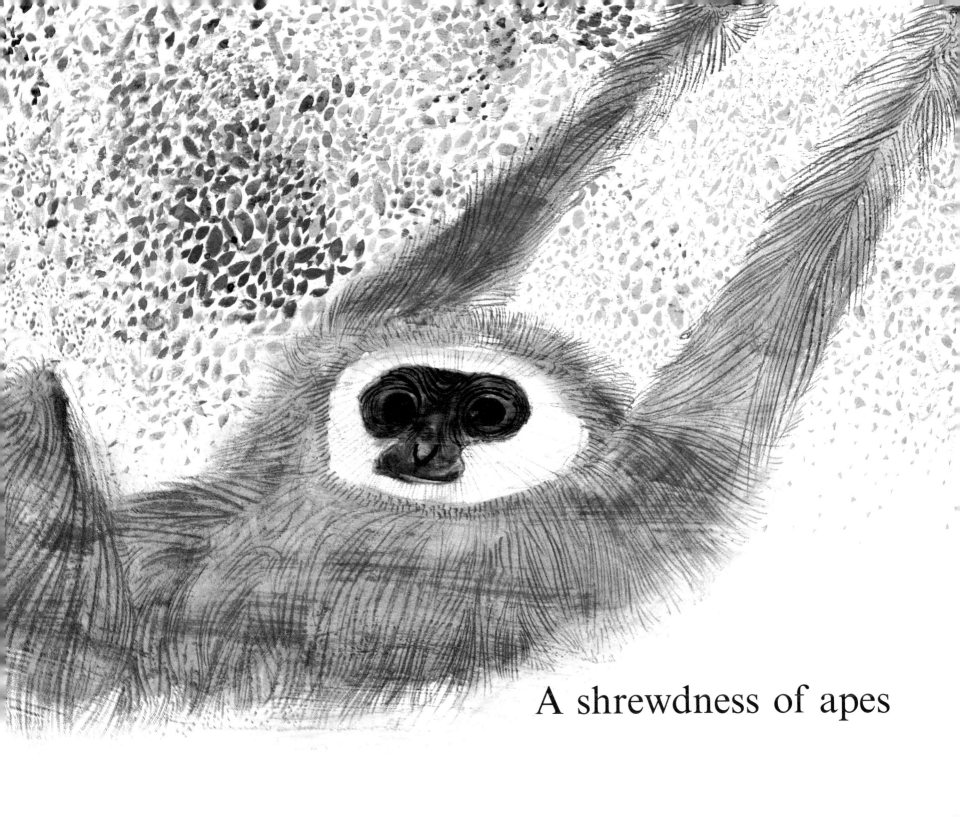

A shrewdness of apes

A pride
of lions

A herd of elephants

A lepe of leopards

A corps of giraffes

A troop of kangaroos

A skulk of foxes

A family of otters

A cete of badgers

An array
of hedgehogs

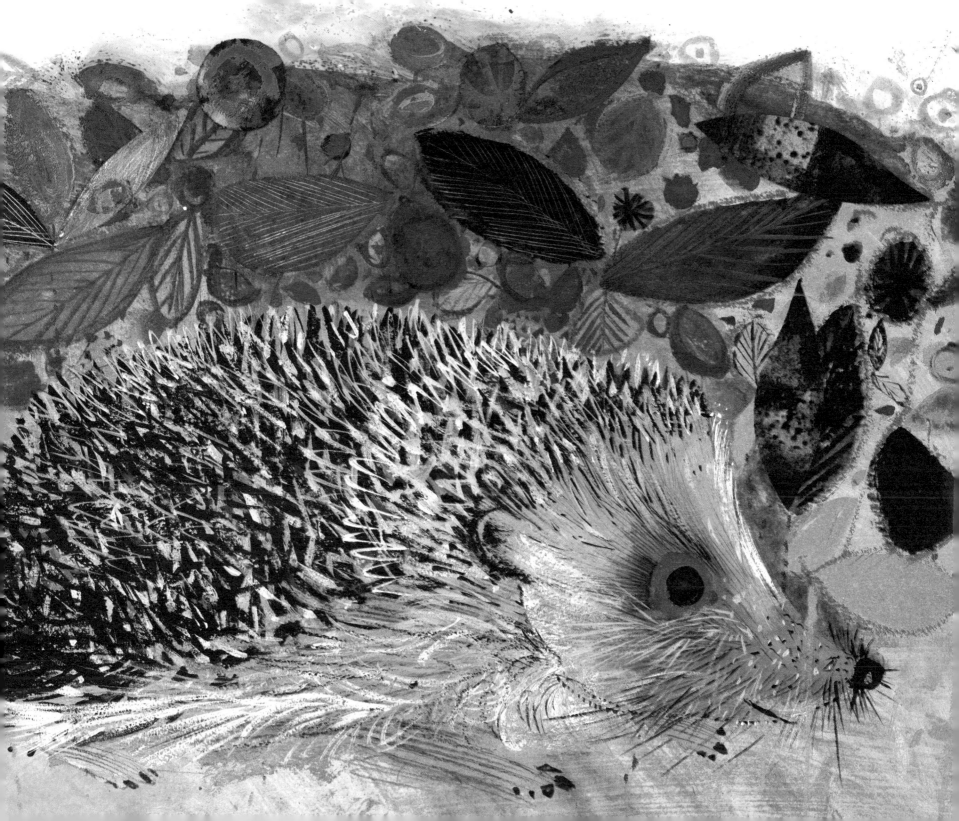

First published 1967 by Oxford University Press
First American publication 1967 by Franklin Watts, Inc.

Library of Congress Catalog Card Number: 67 20869